How To Get Your Ex Back

Effective Psychological Strategies For Reconciling With Your Former Partner And Rekindling Their Affection

(Guidance On Rekindling A Romantic Relationship And Navigating The Healing Process After A Breakup)

Alexis Bellemare

TABLE OF CONTENT

Enhance Your Personal Growth And Development In The Course Of This Journey.....1

Assured Techniques For Rekindling Your Relationship With Your Former Partner..............5

It Is Possible To Successfully Reconcile With Your Former Partner And Regain Their Affection!..14

Reestablishing Connections Through Incremental Measures And Symbolic Actions 18

Ensure Clear And Definitive Understanding Of Your Relationship Goals 26

Presenting Yourself In A New Light And Encouraging Her To Take The Initiative 37

Picking Up The Pieces..44

Remembering The Positives.....................................44

Are You Experiencing Difficulty Moving On From Your Previous Romantic Partner?...........67

Time To Tease...76

Master The Technique Of Relinquishing The Past. 85

What You Need To Change 102

Altering Your Mindset And Strategy 110

The Error Typically Committed By Males Confronting Divorce Proceedings Involving Their Spouse 115

ENHANCE YOUR PERSONAL GROWTH AND DEVELOPMENT IN THE COURSE OF THIS JOURNEY.

Introduction

I would like to express my gratitude and extend my congratulations to you for successfully acquiring the book titled "GET YOUR EX BACK."

This literary composition presents verified methods and approaches to not only facilitate the reconciliation with your former partner, but also foster personal growth and development throughout the journey.

Terminating a romantic partnership can prove to be one of the most challenging aspects within a relationship. Generally, breakups tend to be unfavorable in the majority of cases. There are a plethora of diverse emotions experienced during this process, including anguish, suffering, and occasionally even despondency, among others. There exist a multitude of rationales behind individuals' choice to terminate relationships, yet, in the majority of instances, I believe the ensuing emotional distress is universally comparable. The affection that one develops for an individual with whom they may have shared a significant amount of time shall endure indefinitely. It might likewise represent a nascent relationship, yet you discern the inherent possibilities it holds for future development.

The question at hand is whether it is rational to endeavor towards the reconciliation of a former romantic partner. Should you choose to reconsider reuniting with your former partner after setting aside your emotions, undoubtedly, it would be a highly favorable outcome. On the contrary, should you choose to peruse this book and conclude that it is in your best interest to progress, it would undoubtedly prove to be a wise resolution for your existence as well. It may not invariably serve your ultimate advantage to rekindle a romantic alliance with your former partner, and further discourse on this matter will be presented within the pages of this book. Our primary intention in writing this book was to offer readers valuable guidance and insights that would enable personal growth, regardless of the path they choose when navigating their post-relationship dynamics. It is our conviction that personal growth and self-improvement empower individuals to possess exceptional capabilities, granting them a highly desirable quality of having absolute mastery over their destiny.

Thank you once more for acquiring this book. It is my sincerest hope that you derive great pleasure from its contents.

Assured Techniques For Rekindling Your Relationship With Your Former Partner

Numerous individuals have encountered challenges in swiftly reinstating a former partner into their lives. However, it has been established that there are seven indisputable steps that have been proven to be effective. Direct your attention towards the systematic actions that can be undertaken to ensure a tranquil reunion within a span of three days. Prior to commencing the procedure, allocate a period for personal recuperation through a moment of solemnity. When you perceive someone as crucial to your life, embark on the initial stage of the journey by composing yourself and cultivating an attitude of patience. Transform your being through the application of critical thinking and harness the potential residing within the depths of your subconscious faculties. On the following day, it is imperative that you maintain authenticity, strive for a positive appearance, and exhibit amiability. On the concluding day, assume greater responsibility and embody the qualities of a supportive companion in the relationship.

Step 1. Exercise patience: If your genuine desire is to reconcile with your former partner, it is crucial to proceed gradually and remain mindful of each progression. Commence the interaction with a cordial greeting and a friendly facial expression, demonstrating your ability to maintain an affable demeanor in the presence of the individual in question. Please refrain from excessively exerting influence and attempting to coerce him into a more committed situation when you encounter him.

Merely display a pleasant facial expression and convey a greeting of basic politeness, refraining from any additional gestures or words.

Step 2. Transform yourself: Recall that the process of reconciling with your former partner is not a pleasant undertaking. Engaging in pretense and making false assurances of personal transformation to regain the affection of your partner will only exacerbate the situation. All of your actions should exemplify honesty and authenticity. Exercise restraint and maintain composure, refraining from appearing desperate or losing emotional control. Evidently, your former partner's departure was not influenced by your respective personalities or character traits as individuals. If such were indeed the circumstances, they would not have delayed until now to terminate their relationship. However, it is possible to make alterations to oneself to a certain extent, but it is important to avoid excessive modifications.

Step 3. Exhibit authenticity: In the event of encountering him at a social event, endeavor to initiate a casual conversation while ensuring that you do not convey the impression that he holds utmost significance in your presence. Maintain a predominantly focused connection with your friends while expressing your pleasure in conversing with him or her and your willingness to engage in communication. However, for the time being, maintain a simplistic approach and foster a platonic friendship. In fact, it would not be amiss to engage in casual, light-hearted flirtation with individuals of the opposite gender during social gatherings.

Step 4. Maintain an outward façade: Endeavor to present yourself in the most favorable light in the event of an encounter with him or her. Ensure that you present yourself in a well-groomed and hygienic manner, and actively engage in novel experiences to arouse the individual's curiosity. Maintaining a consistently polished appearance will concurrently enhance one's self-confidence, rendering them considerably more appealing compared to individuals who display minimal self-care. Many gentlemen are greatly attracted to women who possess a strong sense of self-worth and confidence, finding it considerably captivating and enticing. Thus, it is imperative to consistently present oneself in a visually appealing manner regardless of one's location.

Step 5. Exhibit Cordiality: It is advisable to express a few complimentary statements or offer praise to the individual, as long as you genuinely mean what you say and are not fabricating false compliments for the sake of conversation. This has been executed in alignment with your understanding of your former partner. Many males also derive satisfaction from affirming their self-esteem. Therefore, if your aim is to rekindle a romantic relationship with your former partner, it would be advisable to adopt a tactful and benevolent approach when expressing admiration for their olfactory or visual appeal. Do his new trousers or garment appear visually pleasing? Inform the individual but refrain from exaggerating the situation.

Step 6. Exhibit greater accountability: Considering your heightened sense of responsibility in proactively investigating the root causes of the present situation, the passing of time presents you with an extended opportunity to gather your thoughts, forge ahead in your personal journey, and make prudent choices for your future. Within this context there exists a sense of maturity, a desire to pursue what is most optimal. Due to the fact that you have not contacted your former partner. The individual will gain a genuine perception that you are in the process of resolving matters, and there exists a constant apprehension of losing connection with one another should you perceive your partner as having diminished significance. The end of a romantic relationship often serves as a means of assessing the genuineness of one's commitment towards each other. If either party perceives the potential loss of the other, it could lead to a transformation in their conduct.

Step 7. Establish a friendly rapport: Once a suitable period has elapsed, initiate conversation to reminisce about the numerous enjoyable experiences and cherished memories that were shared jointly. A couple enjoys reminiscing about the highlights of that time, which may potentially ignite a spark that they would be reluctant to extinguish. At this juncture, you will have the opportunity to ascertain whether there exists any inclination towards a reunion. Certain individuals may choose to communicate through telephone calls, while others may opt to engage in humorous banter. Meanwhile, a subset of individuals may directly express their intentions without any ambiguity. Irrespective of the chosen method of communication, the underlying message being conveyed is to proceed with caution or at a deliberate pace. Women often hesitate to express this, however, they demonstrate their interest by seeking proximity, staying informed about your achievements, and extending invitations for a walk or visit.

Nevertheless, the underlying message remains consistent: "Proceed with caution."

I kindly advise against hastily considering reconciliation based solely on his or her words. Allow for a gradual development of your relationship, and if you and your partner are genuinely destined to be together, it will unfold organically over time. Below are some suggestions and recommendations on how to regain his affections following the termination of a romantic relationship. The most optimal approach to reconciling with a former partner involves developing a meticulously structured strategy that encompasses not only the process of rekindling the relationship, but also ensuring its enduring stability.

IT IS POSSIBLE татTO SUCCESSFULLY RECONCILE WITH YOUR FORMER PARTNER AND REGAIN THEIR AFFECTION!

Have you recently terminated your romantic relationship with your former partner? If that is indeed the case, it is likely that you are experiencing intense emotional distress accompanied by feelings of confusion and being overwhelmed. You may be experiencing a profound sense of devastation, as though your entire universe has crumbled before your eyes.

You will feel better in time. Although it may not currently appear to be the case, rest assured that you will ultimately overcome the profound anguish you are presently experiencing. You will pull through. Furthermore, should you desire to regain the affections of your former partner, it is indeed within your capabilities to achieve such a reconciliation. There exist efficacious methods to regain his affection.

You can acquire practical, efficient, and proven methodologies to facilitate the reconciliation with your former partner. Utilizing strategies, one can not only endeavor to reconcile with him but also to establish a long-lasting commitment. One can utilize a foolproof technique to captivate their former partner and reignite their affection.

Your former partner is equally experiencing emotional distress and vulnerability as you are. Nevertheless, he is inclined to withhold his. He may try to act as if he is not affected by the break-up. He is differently programmed. He is predisposed to display composed, poised, and unflappable behavior. Even in moments of pain, he maintains a façade of composure and continues to project a sense of normalcy.

A male individual manages personal matters in a distinct manner compared to a female counterpart. You may seek solace in the compassionate embrace of your girlfriends as you confide and express your sorrow to them. In contrast, your former partner will portray themselves as unaffected by the situation.

In order to regain his affections, it is imperative to profoundly understand and connect with his psychological makeup. You have to know how his thoughts and emotions work. It is imperative to understand how to navigate and address his emotionally guarded nature. Having a comprehensive understanding of his thoughts and emotions will significantly enhance the likelihood of achieving reconciliation with him.

Acquire an understanding of the intricacies of the male psyche prior to initiating your endeavor to rekindle affection in your former partner. If you diligently complete your assignments, you will possess significant leverage over your former romantic partner.

Reestablishing Connections Through Incremental Measures And Symbolic Actions

The period of non-communication should have afforded both yourself and your former partner the necessary opportunity to introspect and discern your true desires. In your circumstances, this duration should have additionally contributed to the enhancement of your character, knowledge, and overall personal development. Upon reaching a point where you have deemed yourself prepared to initiate the process of reconnecting with your former partner, it is imperative to adhere to the principle of maintaining a discrete approach.

Undoubtedly, the art of subtlety plays a pivotal role in discerning your subsequent course of action. One should not anticipate that everything will unfold in one's favor upon concluding the period of no contact. That is not how it operates. If anything, it is imperative to exercise greater sensitivity when considering the approach that should be adopted for the entire matter.

For starters, send feelers. These are messages that exhibit an amicable, informal, and non-intimidating nature. The sole matter from which you should abstain is raising any topic associated with your previous romantic involvement or the dissolution of said relationship. Those things can wait. Meanwhile, mitigate the tension and discomfort by directing your efforts towards fostering your friendship.

The following are a few approaches that can assist you:

- Socialize with acquaintances in common. Participate in pursuits that do not necessitate engaging in profound conversations. Such social gatherings can facilitate a reestablishment of comfort and familiarity between the two individuals.

- Leverage the past to your benefit. During one of your informal outings, conceive of a gesture or activity that will serve as a reminder to your former romantic partner of the qualities that initially inspired their affection towards you. If you have previously received compliments for wearing a garment that flattered you or accentuated your features, I encourage you to wear it once more. One could also consider revisiting the establishment where you previously dined. Alternatively, one could choose to embody the intelligent and articulate individual who has captivated their admiration. Utilize the abundant wealth of your recollections filled with positivity and harness their potential to your advantage.

- Enjoy yourself. Don't be too serious. You aim to maintain a lighthearted atmosphere rather than a somber one. Use humor for effect. Maintain an affable demeanor, avoiding confrontational actions.

- Embrace your authenticity. • Remain true to your individuality. • Maintain your originality. • Stay genuine to who you are. • Express your true self. Do not feign to be someone you are not. Engaging in such behavior will merely give the impression to your former partner that you are exerting excessive effort. Have faith in your individuality.

Above all, it is essential to avoid immediately engaging in aggressive actions. As mentioned earlier, the primary objective is to restore trust and foster camaraderie. Do not allow this stage to become obscured by any form of dialogue that you both are not completely at ease discussing at present. Such matters require a considerable amount of time. Please ensure to prioritize the enjoyment of each other's companionship initially. The significant discussion will inevitably occur in due course. You simply have to remain attentive to appropriate signals and be prepared to respond.

'Big talk'

When the moment for the "significant conversation" arises, ensure that you are adequately prepared. It is crucial that you maintain composure and exercise reason throughout the entirety of the situation. Ultimately, one should avoid disrupting the occasion by succumbing to overwhelming emotions.

To make adequate preparations, one can opt either to engage in prior practice or to document the intended content in writing. In the process, be mindful of the intended message you endeavor to convey. It would be most advisable to commence by offering an apology.

Requesting an apology should not be erroneously perceived as an indication of fragility or surrender. Far from it. It simply denotes that you possess a level of emotional maturity that surpasses the indulgence in trivial implications, and emphasizes your recognition of the necessity to express remorse. Request pardon for any shortcomings, inadequacies, or transgressions that have contributed to the strife within the relationship. Be sincere in apologizing.

Lend an ear

Do not turn the entire process into a unilateral endeavor. Extend an attentive listening to your former partner. Pay attention to the content of his or her discourse. Allow him or her the opportunity to express his or her thoughts and emotions. Endeavor to render this conversation as authentic and genuine as feasibly achievable.

At this point, it is imperative for you to demonstrate trust and optimism, as you embark on this decision, with the belief that a favorable outcome will come to fruition. When presented with an opportunity for redemption, grasp it firmly, take hold of it with determination, and value it deeply. Obtaining a second opportunity can prove to be a challenging conquest; being bestowed with such a chance implies that your former partner is open to granting you another opportunity to rectify past mistakes. Solidify the connection of your romantic relationship by ensuring diligent commitment in order to make this opportunity for reconciliation truly worthwhile. Don't squander this opportunity. Please abstain from repeating the same errors that have jeopardized your relationship in previous instances. Finally, guarantee the durability of your relationship by exhibiting mutual respect and unwavering loyalty towards one another. In this manner, your relationship becomes deeply established in a foundation that engenders durability and satisfaction.

ENSURE CLEAR AND DEFINITIVE UNDERSTANDING OF YOUR RELATIONSHIP GOALS

Within this chapter, I kindly propose that you embark upon a course of action that shall greatly assist you in navigating and fostering successful relationships, be they rekindled or initiated anew. I would like you to reflect upon your specific desires and goals regarding a romantic relationship. It is my desire for you to possess a lucid perception of the attributes, behaviors, mannerisms, and emotions that constitute your perception of an ideal male counterpart. Contemplate the sensation that you aspire to experience whenever you are in the company of that gentleman. This holds significant importance because ultimately, regardless of whether you reconcile with your former partner or enter into a new relationship, it is crucial to be involved in a dynamic that genuinely satisfies your genuine desires and requirements. Please consider taking an additional stride and introspect to determine if your former boyfriend genuinely met your ultimate expectations in the context of a romantic relationship. Prior to responding, I implore you to engage in a comprehensive thought process that encompasses both your emotions and intellect.

Contemplate upon your interpersonal connection with him. Consider all the positive experiences and the less favorable moments. Consider the manner in which he conducted himself towards you. Consider your conduct towards him too. Was there a presence of integrity in this relationship? Was there a genuine sense of allure? The primary factor that held utmost significance in this relationship was the establishment of trust. I kindly request that you demonstrate utmost honesty while responding to the following inquiries. It is possible that you are still experiencing emotional distress due to the termination of your relationship. As evident from your expressed desire to reconcile, it is natural for you to shape a narrative that portrays your ex-partner as the ideal match for you. I kindly request that you thoroughly reflect and question whether he truly embodies the ideal partner for you. If you can unequivocally affirm his suitability, let us prepare ourselves for his recovery.

Each situation is unique

It is evident that I do not possess knowledge pertaining to the circumstances surrounding your former romantic partner's transition into the position of your ex. There are potentially numerous factors contributing to his behavior, therefore it is important for you to acknowledge that your situation may require a unique approach compared to individuals seeking reconciliation with their ex-partners under different circumstances. Did you happen to be the individual responsible for departing from his presence? did he leave you? did you cheat? did he cheat? was there abuse? did someone relocate? was it money issues? These are just a few reasons that could have led to your boyfriend becoming your ex. As previously stated, varying circumstances necessitate diverse strategies. In the subsequent chapters, I will present practical guidelines and recommendations pertaining to real-life strategies for reconciling with a former partner. Please make a careful observation and apply the relevant information that is most applicable to your specific circumstance. It is important to bear in mind that certain information contained within this book will be universally applicable. It should be noted that, in most circumstances, there exists a possibility of reconciling with him, irrespective of the underlying reasons for the termination of the relationship. There is only a singular factor that can effectively prevent his return to you, and we will delve into that matter at a subsequent time.

Adhere to the No Contact Rule, Even When Utilizing Social Media Platforms

In the pursuit of reconciling with your former partner, it is advisable to implement the No Contact Rule on various social media platforms, including Facebook. This regulation is particularly assertive, and it possesses the potential to sufficiently startle your former partner, prompting them to reconsider your motives. In due course, they will likely experience a longing for your presence and desire to establish a connection with you again, thus it is advisable to refrain from prolonging your visit beyond an acceptable duration. You can seek assistance from a mentor or explore an e-learning program.

By violating the principle of non-contact, you expose yourself to the possibility of alienating your ex even more. In addition to fostering a sense of distance from your ex, it will also serve to reinstate equilibrium in the power dynamics. Subsequently, you will be required to initiate the entire procedure anew. This proposition holds merit for the betterment of your own interests. Please be mindful that the No Contact Rule pertains to more than just digital communications. This principle extends to offline interactions, encompassing activities such as telephone conversations.

The implementation of the No Contact Rule can serve as a highly effective strategy to help your former partner recognize your contentment and independence in their absence. You will soon realize that your sense of happiness stems from within. Through the deliberate avoidance of social media, you can effectively demonstrate to your former partner that you possess qualities and attributes that make you a desirable candidate for a new relationship. Utilizing this principle will aid you in overcoming the insecurities of your former partner and facilitating their recognition of their inherent worth in your eyes.

It is of utmost importance to adhere to this rule with maximum precision. It boasts a significant rate of success. Nearly 90 percent of individuals who end their relationship do not engage in communication with their former partner for a period of 30 days or longer. The implementation of the No Contact Rule facilitates a swifter recovery process for individuals and empowers them to restore their self-assurance in initiating contact with their former partner. If you are resolute in your desire to reconcile with your former partner, then it may be prudent to give it a try. It is entirely possible to rekindle your ex's affection without engaging in any form of communication.

Develop into an individual of whom you can hold a sense of pride."

When it comes to reconciling with your former partner, tenacity is imperative. However, when we refer to "persistent," we do not imply the act of increasing the frequency of your text messages fourfold every morning or inundating your direct messages with affectionate letters. An abundance of persistence diminishes your perceived worth in the eyes of your former partner. Authentic perseverance necessitates employing strategic approaches and circumventing amateur errors. Keeping this in consideration is an excellent approach to guaranteeing optimal outcomes.

A method to potentially elicit a yearning for reconciliation from your former partner involves harnessing the principles of the law of attraction. The efficacy of this potent principle of attraction lies in its capability to alter an individual's energetic state. Employ the technique of visualizing to manifest the return of your former romantic partner. Place your attention on the positive aspects of your life and disregard any negative ones. It is highly likely that your former partner will express a desire to reconcile with you. This technique can be applied to any challenging scenario. One could also consider the option of recording one's own voice in order to reiterate positive statements to oneself during the period of slumber.

A common error committed by numerous individuals is displaying excessive dependency or being bothersome. Should your former partner express a desire to discontinue your relationship, it is advisable to refrain from promptly entering into a new romantic liaison with another individual. Please exercise patience for a few months and evaluate the available alternatives. If you encounter someone whom you genuinely have affection for, they might be capable of returning your sentiments. By engaging in this action, you have the opportunity to convey to your former partner that your sentiments of affection towards them persist, as well as expressing gratitude for the time shared in your relationship.

Refrain from initiating communication with your former partner for a duration of four weeks. By undertaking this action, you will effectively evoke pleasant memories of the shared experiences with your former partner. Likewise, in the event of personal growth and development, he will find it appealing and alluring. This is a potential approach to reconcile with your former partner. And bear in mind that failure to accomplish this will result in the termination of the relationship.

Presenting Yourself In A New Light And Encouraging Her To Take The Initiative

Reacquiring the affection and love of your former romantic partner undermines the efforts and commitment invested. As noted in the preceding chapters, it is imperative to exert effort towards the transformation of unfavorable aspects of your character, enhance your self-esteem, and prioritize the development of your strengths. However, it is imperative that you fulfill these obligations while also affording her the necessary personal space to process her emotions and come to terms with the recent events.

Although it is indeed accurate that you have personal emotional matters to address, do not allow these circumstances to discourage you from pursuing her reconciliation. Seize this opportunity to capitalize on the physical distance between yourself and the other individual in order to allow her to recognize your value and witness your transformation. The task lies in effectively conveying to her that her affection for you endures, without giving the impression of deliberate effort on your part. This may appear unusual, however, the greater the extent to which one pursues another individual, the more likely that person will perceive one as being desperate and reliant. When one demonstrates a keen desire to reunite with their former girlfriend through an abundance of attention, it is probable that she would perceive such behavior as insincere, and consequently, distance herself further.

Allowing deeds to speak for themselves

What is the precise manner in which you demonstrate your transformation? One cannot merely claim to have transformed when their behavior contradicts those assertions. It must initiate within oneself; a conscious imperative arises, demanding the transformation of one's negative characteristics into positive attributes.

As an illustration, if you have faced repetitive allegations regarding your lack of responsibility, it is incumbent upon you to take action in rectifying the situation. If your interpersonal bonds have been negatively affected by your extensive socializing with your acquaintances, it might be advisable to moderate that particular behavior of yours. Assume complete autonomy over your existence and acquire the skills to proficiently handle your personal matters, financial affairs, and professional obligations. The pivotal aspect lies in rectifying your concerns, not solely to restore her trust, but also as a means of enhancing personal growth.

Jealousy as a strategy

Attempting to incite feelings of jealousy in one's former romantic partner can prove to be a delicate endeavor, particularly for individuals who do not derive satisfaction from causing emotional harm through their actions. Likewise, the utilization of jealousy as a strategic approach can only prove successful if the underlying factor contributing to the dissolution of your relationship does not involve any instance of marital unfaithfulness. However, when considering the grand scheme of affairs, one must carefully evaluate their priorities and underlying intentions. Are you willing to take any action to reconcile with her, or do you intend to passively observe her distancing herself from you?

The effective utilization of jealousy as a means to capture her attention hinges upon its skillful implementation. To begin with, it is important to maintain an air of nonchalance; refraining from parading or excessively focusing on the subject, as doing so may come across as contrived and lackluster. Therefore, when discussing other females in her presence, it is crucial to avoid giving the impression that you have strong romantic inclinations towards them, and refrain from drawing comparisons between them and her. Allow her to witness you engaging in lighthearted interactions with other females, ensuring that you maintain a balance and avoid excessive behavior. The objective is to present yourself in a manner that demonstrates your enjoyment in the presence of others, thereby leading her to acknowledge the extent of the pleasure she is foregoing.

Power of forgiveness

After successfully capturing her attention, refrain from immediately moving in for the final conquest. The passage of time is necessary for these matters, thus it is crucial that you maintain a composed and optimistic demeanor during the entire course of events. Please refrain from hastening, as it will only lead to unfavorable outcomes for you.

Commence with a blank canvas by acknowledging any previous errors and seeking forgiveness. Please exhibit sincerity by accurately articulating your shortcomings, and proffer a legitimate commitment to refrain from repeating them going forward. This commitment should be enhanced by the evident transformation in your behavior and attitude. It is inherent for the young lady to exhibit a degree of apprehensiveness, especially in light of any past adverse experiences, hence, demonstrate unequivocally that there is no basis for her trepidation in considering affording you another opportunity.

After successfully obtaining her agreement to go out with you again, you will have an opportunity to exhibit the extent of your positive transformation. Seize this opportunity to subtly convey your longing for reconciliation. Abstain from engaging in excessive pleas or expressing profound despair; instead, exhibit a demeanor of self-assurance and genuineness in both your speech and behavior. Furthermore, it is advisable to refrain from discussing the grievances of previous experiences. Be engaging and casual. Have fun.

Subsequently, continue to schedule additional meetings until a sense of complete ease and familiarity has been reestablished between both parties. As indicated in the preceding chapters, maintaining consistency is crucial. Therefore, it is imperative that you exhibit unwavering dedication to the alterations you have initiated and uphold your commitment to her.

Picking Up The Pieces

Remembering The Positives

Currently, your relationship has concluded. You have arrived at a pivotal juncture. You have the option to either embark on the path of reconciliation, or you may opt to persist in your pursuit for an ideal partner. Evidently, your engagement with this material indicates a renewed desire to rekindle the romantic aspect of your relationship. Prior to indulging in fantasies of fortuitously encountering each other and experiencing the embrace of your beloved, I suggest taking a moment to contemplate your relationship.

What were the factors that initially led to your attraction to your former partner? What attributes or qualities did you possess that attracted his interest? It is of utmost importance to contemplate the dynamics exhibited during the initial phase of romantic bliss between the pair, as that is the juncture towards which both individuals must endeavor to regress, so as to reignite the flames of passion.

It is highly likely that the routine of your daily life has caused your relationship to lose its romantic essence. The factors that led to your initial feelings of love have become obscured. To reestablish the foundation of your relationship, it is imperative that you extricate yourself from the current state of turmoil.

What specifically drew you to your partner? What aspects of your personality or appearance attracted his attention? Please allocate some time for contemplation to identify the essential attributes that contributed to the success of your relationship. To reestablish your bond, it will be necessary to revisit the factors that initially laid the groundwork for your relationship.

Therefore, it is imperative that you dedicate a significant amount of time to seeking out the favorable aspects within your relationship. Stated differently, what caused your profound affection to develop? Carefully consider and compile them within a written format.

Evaluating the Negatives

Similar to all aspects of life, every relationship has its imperfections. With the passage of time, you will eventually grow weary of the unfavorable aspects and terminate the relationship. This can occasionally be attributed to significant factors like betrayal through extramarital affairs. Relationships may also terminate due to the accumulation of several minor issues over time, such as the inadvertent oversight of a birthday. What were some of the challenges experienced within your interpersonal dynamic?

Please allocate a moment to compile those items presently. At present, it is understandable that you may be experiencing certain adverse emotions which prompt you to make derogatory comments regarding your former partner, such as referring to them as promiscuous or similar expressions. Although you may hold such a perspective, it is important to acknowledge that these unsightly expressions do not accurately portray the issue at hand. You ought to endeavor to adopt a more impartial perspective.

Herein lie a few instances pertaining to the unfavorable aspects within your relationship:

- He was not prepared to establish a long-term commitment.
- Our perspectives on dedication diverged.
- There was a breach of trust within the relationship resulting in unfaithfulness.
- Our values did not align. • Our values were not in harmony. • Our values were incongruent. • Our values diverged. • There was a lack of congruity in our values.

- Our interests and hobbies did not align.

Your list has the potential to vary in length, ranging from an extended roll of tissue paper to a mere solitary sheet. Regardless of the multitude of negative aspects you may identify in your relationship, it is crucial to provide explicit and precise details as you compile your list.

The Deceptions You Engage In with Yourself

I understand that you have recently experienced the dissolution of your romantic relationship. It is a challenging situation, regardless of whether the breakup occurred recently or some time ago, as there is a strong yearning to reconcile. But why? "In the initial phase following the dissolution of the relationship, you might find yourself contemplating numerous justifications for reconciliation and pondering the following thought:

- My survival is contingent on his presence.

- I will not be able to find a more suitable partner than my former significant other.

- My former partner was the sole positive aspect of my life.

- My former partner resolved all of my flaws and imperfections.

- He meant everything to me.

- I am unable to find contentment on my own.

- He was the most significant blessing/advantage that I have ever experienced.

It is customary to experience such emotions; however, it is imperative for you to become aware that all of the aforementioned assertions are fabrications. These are falsehoods that you convince yourself of in order to bolster your emotional well-being. It is indeed possible for you to regain happiness as an individual, regardless of whether this person is present or not.

It is a fact that one's ex's absence does not result in mortal consequences. If he constituted the entirety of your existence, it is imperative that you first work towards enhancing the quality of your own life. One can come across numerous well-qualified individuals by actively engaging with the social sphere. By taking such action, you might even capture the interest of your former partner. Therefore, I implore you to cease the indulgence in self-pity.

5. If he has encountered someone else

It can evoke the sensation of your most dreadful envisioning.

Perhaps you have been informed of this information via informal channels. Alternatively, perhaps he divulged this information to you during the termination of your relationship. Your former partner, who you believed to be your perfect match and envisioned a lifelong commitment with, has transitioned into a new phase of their life. He has encountered another individual.

How is it possible for one to maintain composure amidst excruciating pain?

One may experience a variety of emotional responses. Desperate. Sick with jealousy. Angry or betrayed.

Make a concerted effort to refrain from allowing these emotions to dictate your actions. Recognize their presence, and subsequently endeavor to progress forward. To the best of your abilities, persevere in directing your attention towards your own personal growth and aspirations.

Your acquaintances will be cognizant of the challenges you are facing during this period. They might perceive their actions as supportive, despite engaging in the negative portrayal of his new partner, which entails criticizing her appearance and capabilities in an attempt to instill comfort within you. Kindly request that they refrain from engaging in such behavior. It fosters a sense of resentment within you. Adverse emotional states will pose a substantial impediment to your endeavors to permanently reconcile with your former partner.

Alternatively, endeavor to contemplate his new partner from an objective standpoint. Evaluate their relationship with composure and logical reasoning.

What aspect or qualities does he find attractive or appealing about her?

In what aspect does she distinguish herself from you? In positive, negative, and neutral manners.

What distinguishes their relationship from the one you previously had?

In the event of a substantial dissimilarity between you and her, it might be perceived as corroborative evidence that you and your former partner were incompatible. This possibility exists; however, it does not necessarily hold true. Make a conscious effort to avoid feelings of inadequacy or being replaced. The concept of 'being different' does not necessarily imply superiority.

If your former partner has selected a new companion with substantial dissimilarities from yourself, it could potentially indicate that certain aspects of his character remained unrefined during the duration of your relationship. Perhaps he harbored a modest inclination towards mountain climbing, whereas you gravitated towards more comfortable and leisurely pursuits indoors. He also had an appreciation for days of comfort and warmth. During the duration of your companionship, he never attempted the activity of mountain climbing. It is plausible that he never relayed his interest to you.

Now he has encountered an avid mountaineer. He is experiencing a strong desire for a transformation in his life. In a manner similar to yourself, he is engaging in an exploration of a novel form of existence. All of a sudden, he has devoted himself entirely to the pursuit of mountain climbing.

This does not imply that a mountain climber is his sole or appropriate choice.

Keep in mind: He is also endeavoring to ascertain his requirements and preferences. Occasionally, that necessitates a certain degree of excessive effort. Occasionally, it entails directing his aim towards a contrary course from that which is familiar to him. Over time, similar to the oscillation of a pendulum between extremes, he is expected to find a more moderate stance.

If she exhibits remarkable resemblance to you, it is important to acknowledge the implications without succumbing to excessive enthusiasm. It implies that there are aspects of both you and him that he finds appealing.

Possibly, he simply perceived a necessity for a drastic change. It is possible that he has developed apprehensions regarding his perceived position within the context of their relationship. It is possible that he could have developed concerns or apprehensions pertaining to other aspects of his life, such as familial or occupational matters, and subsequently terminated the relationship in an attempt to regain a sense of control and stability.

However, it is important to continually inquire: What insights can be gained about my former partner from this experience?

Continuously monitor the lists provided in Activity #1. Continuously provide them with updates as you progressively acquire deeper understanding of your former partner, the dynamics of your relationship, and your own emotions. Persist in evaluating if your former partner is truly a suitable individual for your long-term companionship.

If it is your determination that he is still the suitable choice for you, then the query persists: How should you address his recent involvement with another individual?

Progressing your agenda

There is little merit in attempting to euphemize the matter. If your former partner has entered into a new relationship, the task of permanently reconciling with them would become more challenging. Firstly, it is important to acknowledge the reality that there are no assurances. If you are successful in reclaiming his affection, it will undoubtedly require a sustained, protracted effort. A question of several months, perhaps even extending to years.

Are you prepared to commit such a significant amount of time and effort? Alternatively, do you believe it would be more advantageous for you to seek out another individual?

If you sincerely believe that your ex is the ideal partner for you, there are several measures you can initiate to increase the likelihood of successfully reuniting with him in a lasting manner. Primarily, exercise vigilance in how you communicate with your former partner and their current significant other.

Dealing with the unfamiliar counterpart

His new girlfriend may instill a sense of unease or apprehension in you. Alternatively, you may experience feelings of intimidation and unhappiness in her presence.

Bear in mind the guiding principle of your letter of apology: grace.

Please bear in mind that she is likely experiencing a similar sense of vulnerability towards you as you are towards her. She will be informed of the collective history that you and your former partner possess. It is highly likely that she will frequently ponder upon the memories and cherished connection that both of you possessed.

Therefore, one can genuinely astonish their former partner by displaying grace and poise instead of engaging in petty and malicious behavior. When you find yourself in social environments alongside both individuals, it is advisable to exude warmth, kindness, and a sense of humor. Please address her in the same manner you would address him. Make small talk. Inquire about her personal background and attentively attend to her responses. Display charisma, but refrain from excessively flattering her. Refrain from inquiring or extensively questioning her. Do not instill the perception that you are exploiting her as a means to access him.

Furthermore, it is advisable to refrain from expressing admiration or disapproval towards your former partner in her presence. In the event that you are in a solitary situation with your former partner, it is best advised to refrain from expressing either commendation or criticism towards her in his presence. Remain charming, but neutral.

Should you express disapproval towards her, your former partner will interpret it as an expression of jealousy.

If you excessively laud her with effusive praises, it could have adverse consequences. Your former partner will continue to hold your opinion in high regard. This may be interpreted by him as a signal of your sincere belief in the compatibility between the two individuals.

Striking this equilibrium can be challenging. Occasionally, you might inadvertently veer towards one end or the other. However, continue to endeavor to maintain that delicate balance. In order to increase your chances of reconciling with your former partner, it is imperative.

Key tips

First and foremost, it is imperative to keep in mind the initial steps of the program. Allocate resources towards the pursuit of your personal passions and aspirations for personal growth. This will allow you to exhibit politeness while maintaining a certain degree of detachment during your encounters with the three individuals in social settings. Individuals who are consistently engaged and satisfied in their endeavors possess an alluring quality. It is natural for your former partner to ponder upon your current, flourishing existence, and it is desirable for him to contemplate your presence in his thoughts.

Ensure that you are impeccably attired and presented when anticipation of an encounter with him or them arises.

Exercise discretion when deciding the appropriate occasions to reminisce about pleasant memories shared with others, especially when in their presence. The event that both of you attended was truly remarkable. A comedic motion picture that you both viewed as a collective experience. Nothing obviously romantic. Select recollections that will serve as reminders to your former partner of untroubled and joyous moments shared with you.

Be subtle about it. Please refrain from frequently or conspicuously invoking past memories in a manner that may alienate his new partner from the conversation. Your former partner will be highly aware of this, and it will only serve to distance him further.

Please refrain from attempting to undermine his new partner. Please refrain from mocking her, criticizing her, or orchestrating situations that would undermine her dignity. That does not align with the individual you aspire to become.

Refrain from succumbing to the entrapment of assuming the role of the confidant for your former partner, sought out merely for counsel regarding his romantic relationships. Exhibit warmth while maintaining respectful professionalism. You desire him to perceive you as a respected associate rather than someone maternal or a confidante for his romantic affairs. It is unheard of for anyone to accompany the advice columnist.

It is imperative not to engage in attempts to encourage your former partner to engage in infidelity with you, as this goes against ethical standards and the principles of relationships. A man for whom this is effective is not worthy of possessing. In the event that he demonstrates a willingness to engage in deceitful behavior once, it is plausible that he may engage in similar dishonest actions in the future, particularly when the circumstances are reversed.

It will take a considerable amount of time. Occasionally, it may be perceived as agonizingly sluggish. Consider this as the act of sowing seeds, intermittently and at regular intervals. Gradually... Over time, it is your aspiration that they will gradually blossom into a flourishing garden of flowers.

You must allow the flowers to grow at their own natural pace. They require a significant amount of time to reach full maturity and achieve their optimal state of growth. So be patient. Meticulously cultivate your relationship with your former partner, demonstrating great care and utmost sensitivity, akin to tending to a meticulously maintained flower garden. In due course, provided you navigate the situation skillfully, your exertions may eventually yield the desired results.

ARE YOU EXPERIENCING DIFFICULTY MOVING ON FROM YOUR PREVIOUS ROMANTIC PARTNER?

Undoubtedly, As You May Already Be Aware, The Act Of Ending A Relationship Is Invariably Challenging. Furthermore, The Process Of Recuperation Often Proves To Be Significantly More Arduous.

Disengaging From A Significant Relationship Can Pose Considerable Challenges In Terms Of Emotional Recovery, Particularly In Cases Where It Was Not One's Own Volition.

In The Lives Of Adults, Separations Represent One Of The Most Distressing Experiences That We May Encounter.

Certain Individuals May Find That The Process Of Recovering From A Unsuccessful Partnership Persists For A Longer Duration Compared To Others.

Presently, You May Find Yourself In A Situation Where You Experienced A Breakup Quite Some Time Ago, And One Would Expect That You Would Have Overcome It By Now. However, Regrettably, You Still Find Yourself Unable To Do So.

Perchance, You Have Pondered The Inquiry That Leaves Numerous Individuals In A State Of Confusion Following A Romantic Separation As You Strive To Progress, On One Or Two Instances, Which Is; "Why Does It Prove To Be Such A Daunting Task To Overcome The Emotional Attachment To A Former Partner?"

Fortunately, Rest Assured That You Are Not The Inaugural Individual To Encounter Such A Predicament, Nor Will You Be The Ultimate One To Do So. An Innumerable Multitude Of Individuals, Myself Included, Have Overcome Profound Emotional Turmoil, And I Am Confident That You Will Do The Same.

Could You Please Provide An Explanation As To What It Signifies When You Haven't Moved On From Your Previous Romantic Partner?

Does It Imply That You Retain Strong Feelings For Them And Should, Perchance, Make Every Effort To Reconcile And Renew The Relationship?

I Am Of The Opinion That It Is Unlikely. Not Necessarily...

Let Me Explain.

To Begin With, Life Does Not Adhere To The Tropes Often Found In Romantic Comedies.

Typically, Once A Relationship Concludes, It Is Expected To Remain Concluded, Unless There Are Substantial Alterations That Significantly Modify The Circumstances.

If You Continue To Experience Difficulty Moving On From Your Former Partner, It Is Possible That The Underlying Cause Is Influenced Less By Love, And More By Personal Internal Factors.

Given This Circumstance, The Notion Of Not Having Moved On From Your Previous Partner Can Be Interpreted As An Indication That, On A Profound Level, You Have Yet To Fully Acknowledge And Embrace The End Of The Relationship.

Allow Me To Impart My Perspective That One Can Indeed Harbor Affection For A Former Romantic Partner, While Simultaneously Acknowledging The Reality That The Relationship Has Concluded. (Incidentally, This Requires A Considerable Amount Of Resilience And Inner Strength).

Indeed, It Could Be Contended That An Integral Aspect Of Love Encompasses The Ability To Relinquish.

Given That Your Lingering Attachment To Your Ex Does Not Solely Stem From Enduring Affection, What Is The Underlying Cause Preventing You From Moving On?

There Are Multiple Factors That Should Be Mentioned In Relation To This. However, Prior To Disclosing This

Information, Please Allow Me To Impart The Following.

A Recent Study Conducted At Stanford University Revealed That Individuals Experience A Greater Psychological Weight From Rejection When They Perceive That Their True Identity Has Been Disclosed Or Unmasked.

I Strongly Disagreed.

One Can Decidedly Assert That Few Experiences In Life Are As Emotionally Distressing As Being Rejected By An Individual Who Possesses In-Depth Understanding Of Your Character And Subsequently, Inexplicably, Chooses To Retract Their Affection Or Desire To Be In Your Company.

It Is Not Surprising That An Esteemed Psychology Professor At Stanford University, Carol Dweck, Has Articulated, "The Act Of Being Rejected By Someone Who Initially Believed They Loved You, But Later Changed Their Perception Upon Acquiring Additional Information, Can Pose A Significant Threat To One's

Sense Of Self, Leading Individuals To Profoundly Question Their Intrinsic Identity."

In My Personal Opinion, However, I Believe That The Underlying Factors Contributing To An Individual's Inability To Move On From A Former Romantic Partner Can Be More Intricate.

As Previously Indicated, There May Exist Multiple Factors Impeding Your Ability To Progress And Recover From The End Of Your Romantic Relationship.

Upon Achieving An Understanding Of The Potential Obstacles Hindering Your Progress, You Will Then Be Equipped To Proficiently Undertake The Imperative Measures Required To Overcome The State Of Emotional Stagnation.

In A Particular Instance, The Esteemed Progenitor Of The Telephone, Alexander Graham Bell, Expressed The Notion That When One Door Shuts, Another Inevitably Opens. However, Our

Tendency To Contemplate The Closed Door With Feelings Of Longing And Remorse Often Blinds Us To The Existence Of The Newly Opened Door Before Us.

It Is Quite Surprising To Discover That The Inventor Of The Telephone Possessed Such Adeptness In Dispensing Advice That Exhibits Relevance To The Realm Of Romantic Relationships.

Moreover, Overcoming Heartbreak Or The Aftermath Of A Failed Relationship Is Not A Simple Task. According To Shannon Tebb, A Relationship Expert, It Can Be Quite Challenging To Come To Terms With The Fact That Someone No Longer Desires Your Company.

It Can Be Perceived As An Assault On One's Self-Esteem, Giving Rise To A Sense Of Personal Inadequacy.

The Explanation Lies In The Fact That Ourrelationships Constitute An Integral Aspect Of Our Identity. And Undoubtedly, The Loss Of Such Individuals, Particularly Those With

Whom We Share A Close And Personal Bond, Can Significantly Challenge And Unsettle Us On Multiple Levels.

The Loss Of An Intimate Or Longstanding Partner Can Result In A Profound Loss Of Our Sense Of Self. And Devoid Of That, It Is Possible For Us To Be Ensnared Or Even, More Direly, To Be Adrift Amidst Unfavorable Cycles That Perpetuate Our Unhappiness, Fear, And Certainly, Immobility.

If You Find Yourself In A Predicament Characterized By The Aftermath Of A Profoundly Distressing Emotional Disappointment, Wherein You Are Consumed By Thoughts Of A Past Romantic Partner That Persistently Linger In Your Consciousness, It Is Imperative That You Reestablish Your Own Identity And Accomplish This With The Same Level Of Empathy, Affection, And Comprehension That You Would Bestow Upon A Cherished Companion.

The Advantage Lies In The Fact That Through The Acquisition Of Self-

Awareness And Clarity Of Personal Aspirations, One Possesses The Capacity To Redefine Their Life Trajectory, Surmount Obstacles, And Ultimately Emerge From Adversity With Enhanced Resilience And Newfound Happiness.

However, There Is Still One Lingering Question That Has Yet To Be Resolved. And That Is The Reason For Your Hesitation?

Please Join Me In Exploring The Pages And Discovering The Answers Together.

Time To Tease

The art of seduction.

Now that you have obtained the temperature and recorded pertinent particulars, subsequent to your initial intimate encounter, let us proceed to the subsequent phase. Now, you shall endeavor to subtly allure your former partner further. You will make concerted efforts to win back his/her affection by engaging in activities that will elicit an overwhelming sense of joy in him/her.

- If your former partner is of the female gender: - In the case that your previous romantic relationship was with a woman: - Considering the scenario where your ex-partner is a woman: - Given that your past significant other is female in nature:

There exist numerous approaches through which one can capture the affections of a woman. An individual who is either unmarried or currently involved in a romantic partnership may not invariably receive the level of attention to which she is entitled. While it is not expected for you to assume complete control over this particular aspect of her life, you can leverage it to your benefit in the following manner:

- One can employ the traditional approach of wooing a woman, whereby flowers are sent as a token of affection (the quantity of flowers being insignificant, as the essence lies in the kind gesture), accompanied by a thoughtful card and a selection of chocolate. It is commonly observed that women tend to feel a sense of flattery when their former partner still harbors desires for them. In light of this, it is recommended that you translate your sentiments into actions by sending her a curated bouquet of flowers accompanied by a carefully crafted card, wherein you can elucidate your sincere emotions towards her. For example, "such as someone of exceptional qualities" or "such as the person who embodies the love of my life." Furthermore, you have the option to politely request another opportunity to meet and explicitly express it on the accompanying card. Can you imagine the impact on your ex's emotions when she witnesses her colleagues gazing at her with envy? Chocolate has a propensity to soften the heart of a woman. The ingestion of sugar will stimulate neurological processes in her brain which will subsequently elicit uncontrollable physiological responses in her cardiovascular system. It occasionally elicits aphrodisiac-like effects. Your former partner will undoubtedly express gratitude for the bouquet you have graciously bestowed upon them, and they will assuredly accept your invitation for another rendezvous filled with romance.

- You have made an unforeseen and surprising entrance. At what location do you arrive subsequent to concluding your work responsibilities, in light of the information shared during your discussions regarding her place of employment? Do recall the discussion we had earlier regarding refraining from inquiring about personal matters? Once again, I present you with these flowers as a gesture of welcome. Kindly personally deliver them to her. This occurrence consistently brings about a delightful surprise for a woman, as it engenders a sense of uniqueness and importance within her. Do not obstruct the occasion; inquire about her preferences for future plans, such as dining out or attending a film screening.

Allow her to make the selection, granting her the opportunity to preside as the sovereign of the evening.

- If the individual in question happens to be a male with whom you were previously involved in a romantic relationship:

Recall our prior suggestion to opt for a modest activity during the initial appointment, as it was deemed more suitable given the necessity of obtaining his undivided focus. On this occasion, circumstances shall diverge from the previous norm. In many instances, men exhibit a desire to be cared for like young children, suggesting that there is a lingering childlike nature within them. In order to gain insight into an effective approach for captivating his attention, it would be prudent to consider his former desires for birthday gifts or reflect upon his personal interests.

-Elicit a pleasant surprise by extending an invitation for him to attend a sporting event of his choice. Purchase a pair of tickets for an upcoming game and promptly contact him on the day of the event. Inquire about his plans and firmly request that he provide an immediate response, as failing to do so will result in him being unable to attend the game. This is great. You extend an invitation to him and promptly notify him of the invitation on the day designated for the game. This experience elicits a strong sense of thrill and excitement, which provokes an exhilarating surge of adrenaline, appealing to the interests of individuals of all genders. You will observe that following this, the previously observed complicity shall be revived, including the manifestation of emotions in his gaze.

-Engage in a conversation with him via the Skype platform. Many individuals fail to acknowledge this, but it is a commonly observed phenomenon that men invariably hold dear the memories of the women with whom they had a genuine and meaningful connection. It is not feasible to pay an unexpected visit to his residence, however, you can entice him through engaging conversations on Skype. It possesses a level of realism akin to an in-person encounter. And he will not decline, as your initial encounter left such a favorable impression. Be cautious not to exceed the boundaries or push beyond the limits, as it simply represents your endeavor to capture his affections. Please ensure that you appear aesthetically pleasing. Exercise creativity, such as allowing him to tour your premises through the lens of your camera, for example. This should be an open and innocent 'virtual encounter'. Please ensure that you uphold one another's personal boundaries, present yourselves in a composed manner, and engage in an informal discussion for a duration of no longer than ninety minutes. Please refrain from exceeding a duration of ninety minutes, as it is advantageous to pique his interest and encourage a desire for further engagement. Thus, allocate a portion of your time to him during this instance.

Irrespective of gender, the act of seduction remains pivotal in the process of rekindling a romantic relationship with one's former partner. Ensuring undivided attention and focus, it is imperative that any course of action you opt for elicits sole thoughts of you in the mind of your former partner.

Subsequent to your grand endeavor of seduction, a momentous occasion awaits wherein you shall solemnize your bond, once more. Arrange a fresh arrangement for an amorous meeting on Friday evening, and ensure an ample provision of breakfast provisions, as the weekend promises to be an extended period of leisure.

As previously mentioned, upon successfully completing this decisive test of charm, you may now proceed to propose a subsequent rendezvous (ideally, on a weekend). Adhere to the identical set of guidelines that you adhered to initially. Do not behave as if you have already reconciled. During this occasion, you are encouraged to engage in discussions pertaining to general topics, ensuring a sense of authenticity as it revolves around you both enjoying a pleasant moment together. This evening, it is imperative that you reestablish the trust and mutual understanding that characterized your previous relationship. Allow yourself to unwind at a nightclub, a pub, and other similar establishments.

Conclude the evening with a gentle embrace. It will either occur concurrently or you will need to inquire with him/her. It is highly probable that, at this point, he/she will no longer be able to resist your charms.

MASTER THE TECHNIQUE OF RELINQUISHING THE PAST.

Individuals frequently become deeply entangled in their past experiences to the extent that progressing forward may appear insurmountable. A wise individual once stated that in order to experience happiness with another person, it is essential to first cultivate a sense of contentment within oneself. Never have words been more accurate. It is truly disheartening to discover one's solitude and subsequently realize that it is an irrevocable circumstance.

Disregard the events of the past.

The experiences and choices one has made in the past exert a considerable influence on their present approach towards life. This holds true with regard to interconnections. If you consistently engage in a pattern of switching from one romantic partner to another, it is possible that you are approaching relationships in an erroneous manner.

The majority of individuals who encounter difficulties in relationships remain emotionally connected to previous experiences.

Allow me to provide you with a visual representation. You encounter someone with whom you establish a strong connection. As your bond matures, the two of you opt to pursue a romantic relationship. After establishing a dedicated partnership, apprehension arises regarding the potential recurrence of past experiences. It is possible that you have experienced mistreatment, deception, or a combination thereof. You start to harbor unexplained reservations, none of which have been disclosed to you by your current romantic partner. You initiate a process of self-isolation and seclusion. You give up communicating.

This marks the commencement of the final chapter. Over time, you will observe a waning of interest from your companion. Once the individual exits the premises, abruptly thereafter.

Allow me to present a straightforward instruction to acquire knowledge:

Please cease the act of persistently bearing your past burdens. It is not required.

- Cease to allow regret to dominate your life.

- Cease fixating on the constant recollection of the hardships you have previously undergone. The designation of 'the past' is not arbitrary. Do not let it exert influence on either the current moment or the forthcoming times. Be kind to yourself.

- Extend forgiveness towards individuals who may have caused you harm in previous experiences. One will never attain emotional progress if one perpetually harbors apprehension towards experiencing further pain.

Love is an enchanting sentiment. It would be regrettable to miss out on this opportunity due to your inability to relinquish the past. Reflecting upon both the positive and negative events of the past is permissible, however, it is imperative to refrain from carrying the burdensome weight of those experiences. Please acknowledge any injuries you may have sustained or any harm you may have caused to others. Embrace it. What has been accomplished is irreversible.

Therefore, it would be advisable to release it instead of clinging onto it. Dedicate a portion of your time to self-improvement. Grieve if necessary. If necessary, allow yourself to shed tears. Become enraged and engage in disruptive behavior.

Please proceed with the task if it is necessary. Eliminate all detrimental elements that are impeding your progress. Disperse it into the atmosphere, then gesture it away. You have earned it, therefore grant yourself authorization to engage in any activity.

Every individual possesses the inherent entitlement to experience joy and contentment. Incorporate both yourself and your partner. One cannot experience happiness in the company of others without first attaining inner contentment.

It is important to bear in mind that your current position is the result of a natural course of events leading you to where you ought to be. It is ultimately fruitless to dwell upon past events. Let go!

How to Rekindle a Relationship with Your Former Girlfriend, Even if She Expresses Reluctance to Meet with You

There exist numerous strategies at your disposal for reconciling with your former girlfriend, although the majority of them necessitate, at a minimum, her willingness to entertain a phone conversation with you. However, in the scenario where she is not inclined to engage in a conversation with you? Here are a few suggestions you may consider:

Kindly inform her of your continued availability.

Arguably the most expedient method to evoke feelings of jealousy in her would be her realization of your involvement in romantic relationships with other women. Nevertheless, there is a potential for adverse consequences that may arise from this situation. Although she may have begun to feel remorse for losing you, upon learning of your new relationship, she may infer that you have moved on from her and are now actively pursuing new chapters in your life. Hence, ensure that your shared acquaintances are informed of your current status of being unattached. She is bound to acquire this knowledge from them.

Utilize this period of separation as an opportunity to enhance various aspects of your life. Enhance your self-assurance or acquire a novel proficiency. Women greatly admire men who possess strength and confidence!

Compose a heartfelt correspondence expressing your affection towards her.

Neither an electronic mail nor a text message, but rather a genuine, handwritten correspondence. Now you will have a genuine opportunity to articulate your emotions. In the current era of digital communication, there are few gestures as personal as the art of penning a handwritten message. It may appear antiquated as a means of rekindling a relationship with your former partner, however, it proves to be effective. There exists a limited number of women who possess the ability to resist the temptation of opening a meticulously handcrafted piece of correspondence.

Whilst it is highly recommended to express thoughts in one's own words, if one encounters difficulties in determining the appropriate phrasing, seeking inspiration from online examples can be advantageous. Please bear in mind that the visual presentation of the letter holds substantial significance, nearly equivalent to the content it contains. Select elegant stationery, place it into a corresponding envelope, employ authentic sealing wax, and dispatch it.

▢ Maintain a positive and optimistic tone.

When you do have the occasion to converse with her once more, it is advisable to maintain a lighthearted atmosphere. Abstain from excessively expressing remorse for your past actions, pleading for a meeting with her, or engaging in contentious discussions regarding the reasons behind the termination of your relationship. She will likely be disinclined to meet with you if you display emotional instability.

Instead, let it be conveyed that our future encounter promises to be enjoyable, devoid of any servility or petty arguments. If it is feasible, endeavor to elicit laughter from her. Your objective will involve creating an environment where she feels comfortable and safe, enabling her to overcome any reservations that linger from the previous separation.

Should you sincerely desire to reestablish contact with your former partner, despite her lack of response to your calls, rest assured that it is possible to achieve. Enlist the assistance of your mutual acquaintances in informing her of your current single status and steadfastness amidst sorrow. Subsequently, initiate communication by way of a written message to reestablish contact. Exercise caution and diplomacy in all situations, as an imprudent decision could result in unfavorable consequences.

6. Adhere to the "No Contact" principle.

This rule is of utmost importance and adherence to it is imperative if the objective truly is to reconcile with your ex. You have no alternative. This principle essentially asserts that one must sever all forms of communication with their former partner. Please ensure that you disassociate yourself from her on all social media platforms, including Facebook, Instagram, and LinkedIn. Additionally, please refrain from engaging in any form of communication with her, such as text messages or phone calls. You will be undertaking this task for three justified rationales. In the first place, it is necessary for your former partner to develop a sense of longing for your absence. By imposing a period of three to five weeks without communication, you are affording them an opportunity to reflect upon your existence and lament the void left by your absence. Secondly, you need time yourself to heal. It would be advisable for you to undergo a few alterations prior to your forthcoming encounter with your former partner. Finally, it is important to note that your former partner is likely anticipating some form of communication from you. Nevertheless, you will fail to meet their anticipated standards, which will greatly agitate your former partner. This phenomenon can be attributed to fundamental principles of human psychology. It is highly likely that one will experience emotional distress upon realization of being disregarded by another individual. Have you never experienced this sensation?

7. Make Changes

We are discussing both physiological and psychological changes in this context. Given the sizable amount of available space at your disposal, it is now possible for you to fully allocate your time solely toward self-care and personal pursuits. There is no need for you to be concerned about someone else. Therefore, this is the opportune moment to make an investment in oneself.

1. Channel your aggression towards physical fitness: the gym provides an outlet for releasing pent-up frustration. Feel free to vigorously engage with the punching bags to achieve your desired results, as in a few weeks you will undoubtedly exude an impressive

aesthetic. If you are slightly above your ideal weight, now is an opportune moment to shed any excess body fat.

2. Adhere to a dietary regimen: It is difficult to resist the temptation of indulging in a delicious burger. Now is the opportune moment to thoroughly revamp your dietary habits. Consuming a nutritious diet will result in an inherent radiance and vitality in your complexion. You will radiate brilliance reminiscent of a polished diamond!

3. Alter your fashion sense: Venture outdoors and utilize your credit cards for purchases. Buy yourself some fashionable accessories. Change up your style. Purchase fashionable apparel that complements your physique. Peruse Google to peruse the current trends in

fashion. Cease your worries and embrace the realm of fashion!

4. Devote oneself to professional responsibilities: considering the surplus of personal time available, one can utilize these additional hours to dedicate to professional endeavors. A person who achieves success and exhibits independence is universally admired. Furthermore, it is essential for one's own benefit and well-being. Directing your attention towards your professional commitments will facilitate a reduction in your contemplation of your ex-partner, which is precisely the remedy you currently require. You also have the option of establishing your own online business.

5. Adopt a fresh pastime: endeavor to explore novel hobbies. Try more adventurous things like bungee jumping or river rafting. Engage in the culinary arts or horticulture. Just keep yourself busy.

6. Take pleasure in the moments: While it is acceptable to experience sadness, be steadfast in not allowing it to engulf you. You should spend time socializing with your peers and engaging in recreational activities. Share photographs of yourself on your Facebook profile and make the most of the experience. You are not obligated to provide any further justifications to anyone. You possess the same level of freedom as a avian creature.

What You Need To Change

Before you can reconcile with your former partner, it is imperative that you reclaim and restore your personal identity.

Allow me to present the steps to accomplish this task.

NOTABLE ENHANCEMENTS TO YOUR PHYSICAL APPEARANCE

Effecting a favorable transformation in your bodily appearance will bestow upon you a rejuvenated aesthetic. You will experience a sense of novelty and enhanced well-being.

When your former partner encounters you following the cessation of communication, they will discern a transformed individual.

Presented herein are several activities that you can engage in.

Get a haircut. Simply consult a professional hairstylist to obtain information regarding the current trends and styles.

Get your teeth cleaned. An aesthetically pleasing smile exudes a strong allure.

Achieve peak physical condition. Proceed to the fitness center and engage in physical exercise to perspire and release tension. This is also beneficial for your mental well-being as engaging in physical activity triggers the release of endorphins, resulting in a heightened sense of happiness.

Get new clothes. They will enhance your sense of self-worth.

I strongly advise against taking any drastic actions at this moment. It is prudent to exercise caution in avoiding any permanent alterations to your physical appearance at present, such as obtaining a tattoo depicting a broken heart, as there is a risk of enduring regret throughout your lifetime.

NOTABLE IMPROVEMENTS IN YOUR PSYCHOLOGICAL OUTLOOK

Cultivating contentment and self-assurance is arguably paramount when endeavoring to reconcile with a former romantic partner.

It is imperative to acknowledge that acquiring happiness and confidence necessitates dedicated efforts towards self-improvement.

Presented herein are several recommendations that can facilitate the development of self-assurance and foster a sense of contentment within an individual.

"How to find happiness independent of your former partner"

Rather than remaining at home indulging in ice cream and television, venture outside and engage in activities that contribute to your emotional well-being.

Allocate a period for yourself to grieve. I am cognizant of the immense difficulty in finding happiness post a romantic separation. I recall being in a state of utter distress for a minimum duration of two weeks. I experienced a lack of restful sleep, inadequate dietary intake, and a preoccupation with thoughts of my former partner throughout the day. To a certain extent, this phase is crucial for your growth/development. You dedicate a portion of each day to grieving. Should you desire to experience feelings of unhappiness and self-pity, feel free to proceed with such course of action. However, it is imperative that you engage in activities that contribute to nurturing a sense of self-worth.

Write in a journal. Please document your thoughts and feelings in writing. Writing can be seen as a form of therapy that undoubtedly aids in the expression of pent-up emotions. Research has indicated that the practice of engaging in expressive writing can be highly effective in restoring a sense of tranquility amidst challenging circumstances.

Go out with buddies. Allocate time to be in the presence of those dear to you. Your loved ones and close acquaintances are the individuals who consistently provide unwavering support and derive joy from sharing moments in your presence. Go out and have a wonderful time with them.

Do some meditation. Be conscious of oneself. Be cognizant of your limitations and abilities. Be proud of yourself. Embrace and acknowledge your true self. That is the essence of self-assurance. The quality of being needy (which is deemed unappealing) arises from internal insecurities. In light of the fact that confidence is derived from acquiring knowledge and embracing self-acceptance.

Engage in a romantic outing together. It is imperative, and should you find yourself perusing this message, I would strongly recommend embarking on a series of dates prior to definitively severing ties with your former partner. It is imperative that you gain a fresh perspective immediately, and from my vantage point, engaging with unfamiliar individuals is the optimal means to accomplish this.

Favorable alterations in your conduct and routines

In many instances, it is your established patterns or behavioral choices that have brought your former partner to the precipice of ending the relationship. If you are facing challenges that may have contributed to the dissolution of your relationship, it is opportune to address them now. Several examples of these challenges encompass.

ALTERING YOUR MINDSET AND STRATEGY

Herein lies the crux of the matter—your progress shall forever remain stagnant unless you alter your approach. This realization is indeed quite challenging, as it requires acknowledging one's own limitations. This is not to imply that you are solely responsible for the occurrence of the breakup. The success or failure of a relationship is contingent upon the contributions of both parties involved, therefore it is crucial to remember this. There is nevertheless something that you are likely desiring to alter, and now you have the chance to accomplish precisely that.

If your objective is to reconcile with your former partner, it is imperative that you prioritize self-improvement as a primary step. This implies modifying your disposition towards this individual and your approach to the possibility of reconciliation. If you desire them and are pursuing them, it will be necessary for you to deviate from the established routine. This will not only entail a repetition of the same outcome, but also render you susceptible and exposed to potential risk. It is imperative to redirect our attention towards the desired outcome that you genuinely aspire to accomplish in this context. If you desire the return of your former partner, it is imperative that you afford them the opportunity to take initiative.

Do not allow this to revolve around others, instead prioritize yourself for once." "Shift the focus away from them and concentrate on your own well-being." "Direct your attention towards yourself, disregarding their involvement.

Cease entertaining the notion that you are reliant upon them, for this erroneous mindset will prove detrimental to your progress. Begin contemplating the myriad of potential opportunities that lie ahead and endeavor to explore the world to a certain extent. Devote some time to self-care and enjoy yourself! Regard this as a novel chance to begin anew and truly define the kind of individual you aspire to become.

As you engage in personal growth and endeavor to cultivate a more optimistic and proactive demeanor, you are temporarily shifting your focus away from them. Subsequently, when they initiate contact with you, a scenario that is highly likely to occur, you are significantly more inclined to allow them to take the initiative and assume the responsibility. This entire procedure might necessitate considerable self-reassurance and engaging in internal dialogue. I am self-sufficient in my endeavors, and his presence is not necessary to achieve my goals.

This pertains to the development of your self-assurance, the cultivation of a positive mindset, and gaining clarity on the critical areas requiring your attention for progress. Please take whatever actions are necessary to temporarily set aside your ex-partner. While this may appear paradoxical, the most effective approach in the long term is to prioritize your own well-being in order to regain their attention. Alter your demeanor and seize this opportunity to embrace the type of position that you desire. It will be advantageous for you to retrieve them, as doing so will greatly enhance the viability of the relationship. View this as a chance for personal growth—and you'll appreciate it when you realize it rekindles your former partner's interest.

THE ERROR TYPICALLY COMMITTED BY MALES CONFRONTING DIVORCE PROCEEDINGS INVOLVING THEIR SPOUSE

It is imperative that we ensure the timely payment of marital expenses. Furthermore, given your independent financial obligations, careful consideration must be given to your affordability. It is possible that you may find yourself in a situation wherein your spouse has full access to all the amenities in the house, while you reside in a smaller place that may not even be under your ownership. Perhaps you are considering a rental arrangement of a relatively brief duration, which may prompt you to reflect upon the merits of a more extended tenure. If you opt for the short-term, what are the expenses associated with it? If you have been committed to a long-term arrangement, may I inquire as to the duration of your previous rental or lease agreement, as well as the expenses incurred in terminating said agreement prematurely?

Should the need arise and one finds themselves in a circumstance where our attention is directed towards ensuring that the financial obligations pertaining to marriage, such as utility bills and mortgage payments, are duly fulfilled. What is your true financial capacity? Thus, you find yourself in that particular circumstance. In a formal tone, you could say: "In this scenario, your spouse resides in the abode, which offers a range of amenities such as a comfortable bed, a well-equipped refrigerator, and other essential facilities. Conversely, you may find yourself inhabiting a comparably smaller dwelling, resting upon a basic mattress, and lacking in material possessions, as your primary focus lies in ensuring the timely payment of expenses."

An additional concern may also arise. If you were to relocate, it could potentially convey to the court that you agree to relinquish ownership of the house to your spouse, while deep down you may have a strong desire to retain possession of it.

That particular property or dwelling. Something worth considering if you decide to relocate is whether it would result in granting your spouse greater leverage in that specific situation. Additionally, as previously mentioned, there would be the additional burden of dual expenses to contend with, further impacting your financial situation. Establishing legal precedents that will be examined by the judiciary, potentially leading to the inference that if the father has voluntarily vacated the premises, it can be inferred that he is in agreement with the situation.

www.ingramcontent.com/pod-product-compliance
Lightning Source LLC
Chambersburg PA
CBHW050256120526
44590CB00016B/2372